2 CORINTHIANS

LIFE-TRANSFORMING GRACE

10 Publishing
a division of 10 of those.com

First published in Great Britain in 2021

British Library Cataloguing in Publication Data
A record for this book is available from the British Library

ISBN: 978-1-913278-20-5
Designed by Diane Warnes
Printed in the UK

10Publishing, a division of 10ofthose.com
Unit C, Tomlinson Road, Leyland, PR25 2DY, England
Email: info@10ofthose.com
Website: www.10ofthose.com

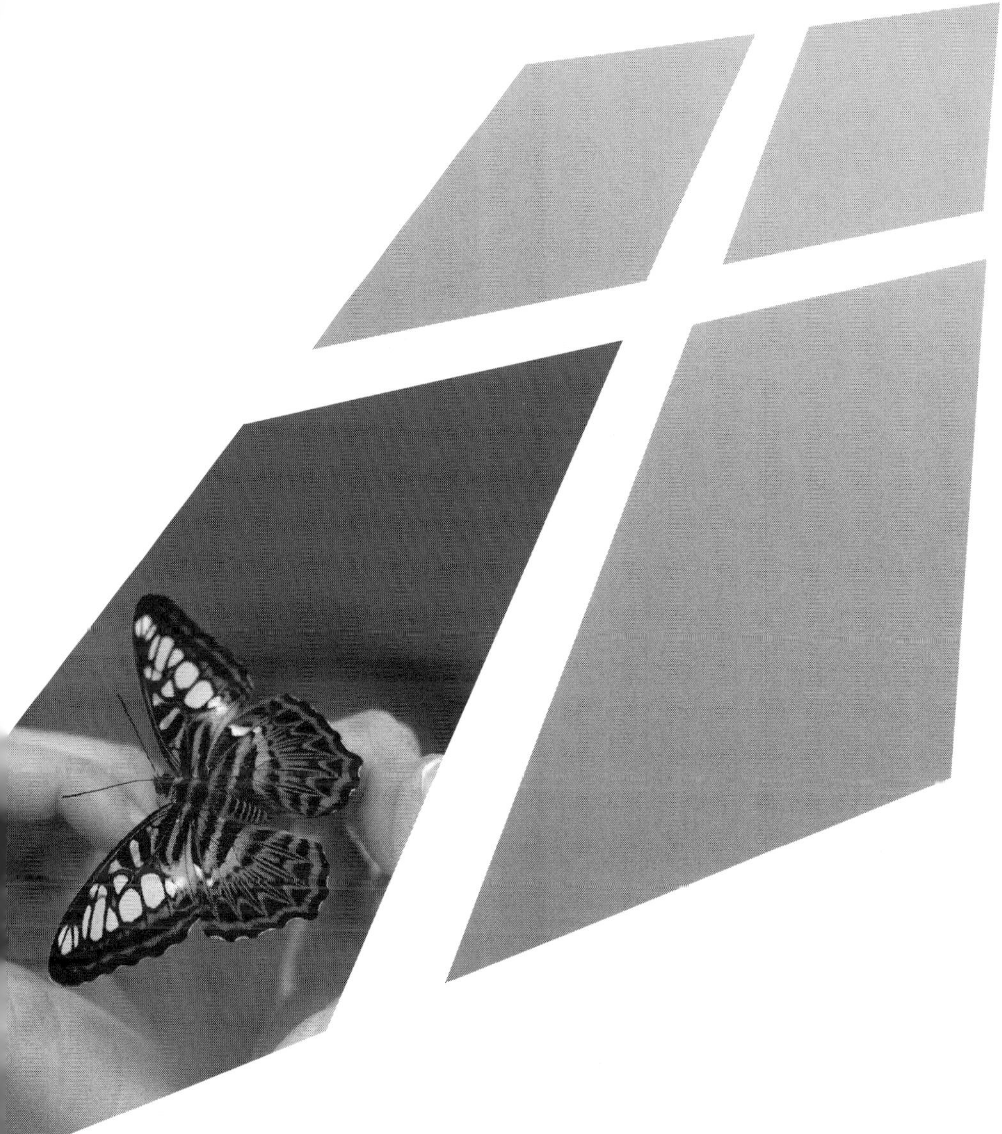

Neil Todman

27 UNDATED DEVOTIONS THROUGH THE BOOK OF 2 CORINTHIANS

DAY 1

READ 2 Corinthians 1:1–2

No church gave the Apostle Paul more problems than the one he planted in Corinth. Yet Paul loved the believers in that corrupt city passionately and wanted the very best for them in Christ. He was like a concerned father who can see his teenage son repeatedly going off the rails and does everything in his power to show him a better way.

Paul wrote to the Corinthians at least four times and visited them on several occasions. His first and third letters are lost to us, but we know his second and fourth as 1 and 2 Corinthians.

The final letter, 2 Corinthians, was written after the relationship between Paul and the church in Corinth had almost completely broken down. Timothy had delivered 1 Corinthians, but the church rejected him and Paul's message. So the Apostle had gone in person to Corinth, but that was a painful visit (2:1) and was followed up with a further letter written out of the anguish of Paul's heart (2:3–4). Paul decided not to return to Corinth until their attitude towards him as an Apostle had changed. Instead, he sent his trouble-shooter, Titus. When Paul and Titus rendezvoused months later in Macedonia, there was finally some good news. Titus was able to encourage Paul that the majority of the Corinthians had repented of their hostility towards him and were ready to obey Christ (7:5–7). 2 Corinthians 1–9 were written on the back of this positive report, before Paul probably received more bad news from Corinth, which may well explain the abrupt change of tone in chapters 10 to 13.

Because of God's grace towards them, neither Paul nor Timothy had given up on the church in Corinth. God's undeserved gifts of love through the cross of Jesus Christ bring us not only peace with our Father God but the basis for reconciliation with others in his family. May grace and peace from God our Father and the Lord Jesus Christ transform our lives daily.

REFLECTION

Give thanks for those who first explained the gospel to you and those who have stood by you at times when you have struggled in your Christian walk.

DAY 2

READ 2 Corinthians 1:3–11 (part 1)

If we live long enough, we will suffer. Being a follower of Christ doesn't give us a deflector shield so that times of trouble will bounce off us, but it does give us something even better: the guarantee that, no matter how tough life gets, God himself will comfort us through his Spirit and his people.

In these verses, Paul doesn't minimise the distress he felt. He repeatedly uses the words for affliction (vv. 4, 6, 8) and suffering (vv. 5, 6, 7). Verses 8 and 9 are heart-breaking. Paul has reached the end of himself. He doesn't know if he can carry on. His life feels like a ship sinking because it is weighed down with too much cargo. Paul's burdens feel too much to bear. Death would be a relief.

I wonder if you have ever felt that way? At points in my life I have, especially when my first wife, Elaine, died aged forty-two following a twenty-month battle with bowel cancer. What can help us when we go through the worst of times?

Paul tells us the answer here in the opening verses of this letter. The most repeated word isn't affliction or suffering but comfort. He uses it ten times, in the original Greek, in verses 4 to 7. We come to the God of all comfort, the Father who shows mercy to us in all our weakest moments (vv. 3–4). We come to Jesus Christ, his Son, the suffering King, who went through the worst of sufferings before being raised from death to life (vv. 3, 5, 9). When we suffer, his death and resurrection give us hope. Even suffering which ends in death will not have the final word (vv. 9–10). And we come to God the Spirit, whom Jesus called 'the Comforter' (John 16:7, KJV), who teaches us to depend upon God and his Word. Father, Son and Holy Spirit give us powerful grace to grow closer to our God through the worst of times.

REFLECTION

During times when you have suffered, which promises from God's Word has his Spirit made precious to you?

DAY 3

READ 2 Corinthians 1:3–11 (part 2)

In the previous reflection on these verses, we considered how, even in the worst of afflictions, our God can comfort us by drawing us into a deeper, more dependent relationship with himself. One way our Father does this is through his Holy Spirit, whom Jesus called 'the Comforter'. Another way, which Paul focuses on here, is through his people.

When we suffer, it can sometimes feel meaningless. We may well wonder why God, who loved us so much he gave his one and only Son to die for us, has allowed such terrible affliction to come into our lives. But verse 4 tells us one of God's purposes in allowing us to suffer: 'so that we can comfort those in any trouble'. Our experience, particularly of the ways God has carried us through the toughest of times, can be a tremendous encouragement to others wondering how they will get through a similar experience.

When my first wife, Elaine, was diagnosed with terminal cancer, my brother brought comfort to me by saying that grace for Christians is like the manna God provided for the people of Israel living in the desert: we get just enough for each day to sustain us. My brother's words meant even more because he had also lost his first wife, Sarah, to cancer. He was further down the narrow road Jesus was now calling me to travel. He pointed me to Jesus.

That's the point of verse 6. Whether those we love in the Christian family are suffering or are comforted, we can learn from their example that God's grace is always sufficient. We can learn to patiently endure through trials because suffering never has the final word.

Finally, in verse 11, Paul reminds the Corinthians of one thing we should always do when we hear those we love are in distress. We should pray for them, always believing God will bless them even in the darkest times.

REFLECTION

Who do you know that is suffering right now? Pray for them. If it is appropriate, why not also send them a card saying that you are praying, and sharing one promise from the Bible.

DAY 4

READ 2 Corinthians 1:12 – 2:4

In the year before 2 Corinthians was written, the relationship between Paul and the church in Corinth had been strained almost to breaking point. 2:1–4 show how difficult things had become. Paul had no longer felt free to visit Corinth, as 1:16 tells us he had intended to do, because his last trip there had been so poorly received. It broke his heart to see the church he had planted so hostile towards him. While there is great joy in loving Christian fellowship, when there is tension, criticism or even public arguments, the reverse is true: there is unimaginable sorrow. No wonder Paul wrote to the church, a letter which we no longer have, with anguish and tears!

As a result, there was a lack of trust towards Paul from some in Corinth. They were suspicious of his motives when he changed his travel plans and accused him of being double-minded, vacillating and duplicitous (1:13, 17).

Paul can't allow this criticism to stand because if his integrity is undermined, it would also undermine the credibility of the life-transforming gospel he preaches. It is essential for the Corinthians to know that Paul and his team live out what they proclaim about Christ. The Corinthians had already found these things Paul had taught them to be true: that God is faithful to his Word (1:18); that in Christ all God's new covenant promises are irrevocable (1:19–21); and that through the Spirit believers are guaranteed heaven (1:22). Similarly Paul's word can be trusted.

In addition Paul makes it clear the Corinthians have not fully understood his motivation in changing his travel plans (1:12–14). It was to spare them the sorrow Paul so acutely felt (1:23) and instead give the church time to find a renewed delight in their eternal fellowship with Paul's team (1:14).

REFLECTION

Why do you think Christians sometimes fall out with one another? What can we learn from this passage about restoring broken relationships?

DAY 5

READ 2 Corinthians 2:5–11

Church discipline isn't practised in many churches today. We have our own distorted notion of what God's love for his people should be like, forgetting that Christ's goal in loving his church is to make her holy (Eph. 5:25–27). Sin must be lovingly dealt with.

It was Jesus who first spoke about dealing with sin among his people and what to do if someone was unrepentant (Mt. 18:15–17). His words were taken seriously by his Apostles (Acts 5:1–11; 8:17–24; Gal. 6:1; Eph. 5:11; 2 Thes. 3:14–15; Tit. 3:10; Heb. 12:4–13).

We can see from these references that church disciple has three main purposes. It is to:

1. maintain the purity of the church.
2. allow the church to be a distinctive witness to the world around it.
3. bring those trapped in sin to repentance and back into useful service of God among his people.

This type of discipline was certainly needed among the Christians in Corinth. In 1 Corinthians 5:1–13, Paul was appalled that the church not only hadn't dealt with a case of incest, where a man was sleeping with his stepmother, but boastfully endorsed his evil behaviour.

In 2 Corinthians 2:5–11, the church has swung the other way. They are refusing to bring a repentant man back into fellowship.

It seems likely this man's offence was against Paul (v. 5). Possibly he was one of the ringleaders undermining Paul's authority as an Apostle. Paul wrote to the church (probably in the letter lost to us but mentioned in verse 4), calling on them to discipline this man (v. 9), and their actions worked (v. 6). Now Paul has forgiven this man (v. 10), so the church must forgive, comfort and love him (vv. 7–8). To not do so would be to hand victory to Satan, because it would look as if this man's sin was unforgivable by Jesus (v. 11).

REFLECTION

Give thanks for those who have loved you enough to confront sin in your life. Pray that your local church leaders would have courage to apply biblical church discipline to those entrusted by Jesus to their care.

DAY 6

READ 2 Corinthians 2:12–17

Until this point in 2 Corinthians, Paul had been mopping up some ongoing misunderstandings between him and the believers in Corinth. But, having cleared the decks, Paul will begin to explain how he knows the attitude of the majority of the Corinthian believers has changed towards him (3:2–3).

First, in verses 12 and 13, Paul updates the church on his preaching itinerary. Once he finished several very fruitful years in Ephesus, Paul was forced to move on (Acts 19:1 - 20:1). Unsafe in Ephesus, and unwelcome in Corinth, Paul instead went to Troas to rendezvous with Titus. But, despite ongoing effectiveness as he preached the gospel of Christ, Paul felt compelled to move onto Macedonia because there was no sign of Titus in Troas (vv. 12–13).

At this point, Paul breaks from explaining how he and Titus were reunited, completing that story in 7:5–7, and instead spends four chapters outlining his ministry for Jesus Christ under the new covenant.

Paul begins in verse 14 with an image that would have been very familiar to anyone living in the Roman Empire. When a triumphant general returned from a successful military campaign, there would be a parade. Prisoners would be led through the streets by the victorious army, before being slaughtered in the arena by wild beasts. Priests would accompany the procession, burning incense to the gods, thus creating a powerful aroma.

Paul applies these events - which caused great celebration for some, while heralding doom for others - to his own ministry. He sees himself as a captive of King Jesus, in the sense that his life belongs to Christ; he would willingly die for him and all glory must go to him. As Paul preaches the gospel, some are saved, while others are hardened in their hatred towards his King (vv. 15–16). Whatever the response, Paul gives himself completely to this work, knowing he is sent by God (v. 17).

REFLECTION

Pray for courage to speak up for King Jesus today, sticking to the message of the gospel whether it is met with openness or hostility.

DAY 7

READ 2 Corinthians 3:1–6

If someone applies for a new job, usually references are taken from previous employers. It is a way of checking whether the applicant comes recommended.

It seems as if some in Corinth thought a similar approach might help rebuild the relationship between Paul and the church. They thought a letter bigging up Paul's credentials, either written by those in the church who knew him best or by respected people outside of Corinth – maybe the Apostles in Jerusalem – would be just the ticket (v. 1).

Paul is appalled! The Corinthian believers are his letters of recommendation, validating the power of the gospel of Jesus Christ that Paul preached to them by the transformation of their lives. Everyone they meet can see they are different people to the ones they were before they met Christ. That is all the evidence needed that the Spirit of the living God is at work in their hearts (vv. 2–3).

In verses 4 and 5, Paul explains that just as he doesn't need his competence confirmed by others, so he doesn't need to complete a self-assessment form. He is answerable only before God for the ministry entrusted to him. God himself has equipped Paul for this otherwise humanly-impossible task: of seeing spiritually dead people brought to eternal life (v. 6).

That is what being a minister of the new covenant is all about. In the Old Testament, God promised through the prophet Jeremiah that he would establish a new covenant with his people, writing his law on their hearts, forgiving their sins and bringing them into a loving relationship with himself (Jer. 31:31–34). Through Jesus' death, our sins are forgiven – a new covenant in his blood has begun (Mt. 26:28). Through the power of Jesus' resurrection, the Spirit gives us new life, with a new desire to obey God from our heart and tell others about him.

REFLECTION

Read Jeremiah 31:31–34 slowly, pausing after each verse to thank God for the benefits of the new covenant brought to you through Jesus Christ.

DAY 8

READ 2 Corinthians 3:7–18

Paul wrote 2 Corinthians to rebuild his apostolic relationship with the church which had been severely damaged by his critics. One area in which Paul faced constant criticism throughout his ministry was his attitude to the Old Testament law given to Israel through Moses. Many felt Paul advocated a lawless Christianity which permitted sin and failed to promote holy living. They thought the lives of Christians following his teaching would be indistinct from those outside of the church. Surely Christians need rules too?

In this passage, Paul begins by showing how rules – even the very best ones – have never transformed one human heart. Verse 7 says that the tablets of stone, which Moses brought down from Mount Sinai inscribed with the Ten Commandments (Ex. 20; 32:15–16), displayed the glory of God. Those commandments revealed the character of God in ways that were unknown before. But the consequence of that was to expose just how sinful all human beings are before a holy God. Judged against that law, no one is righteous, not even one. All deserve death.

However, the law prepared the way for the new covenant in Christ. The law was a temporary measure, albeit lasting 1500 years, before being permanently replaced by an even greater revelation of God's holiness and his mercy: Jesus Christ. Those who deserve condemnation are made righteous through Jesus' death on the cross and the resurrection power given to us by his Spirit.

Under the old covenant, only Moses showed the glory of God (Ex. 34:29–35). In contrast, under the new covenant, all Christians can enter into God's presence, contemplate the wonder of what he has done for us in Christ, and through his Spirit display more of his glorious and gracious character to the world around us.

This truth is still hidden from many. Do you believe it?

REFLECTION

Thank God for some of the ways his glory, revealed in Christ and made real to you by his Spirit, has already transformed your life.

DAY 9

READ 2 Corinthians 4:1–12

Evangelism can be very discouraging. When we pluck up the courage to talk about Jesus, people often respond with apathy or hostility. As a result of what can seem like repeated failures, we may have lost heart and rarely mention our faith in Jesus.

Paul knew what it was to face discouragements. He lists just how tough his life felt in verses 8 to 12. Speaking up for Jesus cost Paul again and again. Yet, despite all these challenges, he says, 'we do not lose heart' (v. 1). What lessons can we learn from Paul's example?

1. We are not at liberty to change the message of the gospel (v. 2)

When faced with hostility, it is tempting to preach a watered-down gospel, with less emphasis on God's wrath and the consequences of unbelief. When faced with apathy, it is tempting to use hype or even manipulative strategies to try to get a more positive response. Neither will do. Like Paul we need to set forth the truth of the gospel plainly.

2. We are not able to change people's response to the gospel (vv. 3–4)

Unless God removes the veil, people are unable to see how wonderful Jesus is and how desperately they need him. It is not just their own ignorance or rebelliousness that keeps them from Christ. Satan, the god of this age, is actively working to snatch God's Word from them before they can respond (see Jesus' words in Mark 4:14–15).

3. We are not to present ourselves but display God's glory in the gospel (vv. 5–7)

Paul has stopped caring what people think about him. He is criticised for being unimpressive (10:10), but he accepts that. He says the treasure God has given him is in jars of clay, the first-century equivalent of carrier bags. This is so that nobody would get caught up with the one presenting the message, but would instead see the light and power of Christ.

REFLECTION

Ask God to give you an opportunity to talk plainly about Jesus today.

DAY 10

READ 2 Corinthians 4:13–18

When my first wife, Elaine, knew that she was terminally ill, she memorised over thirty passages of Scripture so that once she became too sick to read her Bible, she would still have God's Word in her heart. Verses 16 to 18 of today's passage were among the most precious to her. As she struggled with the incapacitating pain of cancer and the grief of saying 'goodbye' to our two primary-school-aged sons, she knew Jesus was renewing her inwardly day by day. His Spirit was making her ever more sure of the eternal glory Jesus won for her through his death and resurrection. The lessons she learnt through cancer, the Apostle Paul had already learned nearly two thousand years earlier in the sufferings he faced.

In this chapter, Paul has already testified to the sustaining grace of Jesus in 4:8–10. Paul is hard pressed, perplexed, persecuted and struck down *but not* crushed, in despair, abandoned or destroyed because of the life of Jesus within him. Alone, Paul's sufferings would have overwhelmed him. With Jesus, he has the strength to carry on with his new covenant ministry.

But crucial to Paul enduring endless troubles, and continuing to boldly preach the gospel, is his eternal perspective. We see this motivation in verses 13 to 15, where Paul says all those who trust in the Lord Jesus will be raised, as Christ was, and presented to his Father. Each individual is a trophy of grace, resulting in endless thanksgiving to the glory of God, who reveals the wonder of his grace by saving sinners.

In verses 16 to 18, Paul weighs his sufferings now in the light of the eternal glory to come. He is fixated by the thought that, no matter how great his troubles may be, they will soon be over. Then he will see Jesus, whose glory far outweighs everything, and be with him forever.

REFLECTION

On the night he was betrayed, Jesus prayed that you would see his glory (John 17:24). Ask God to help you fix your eyes on what is unseen.

DAY 11

READ 2 Corinthians 5:1–10

Living as a Christian in this fallen world isn't easy. In addition to all the troubles everybody experiences at times, if we faithfully tell others about Jesus, we will also face hostility.

In 2 Corinthians, Paul is honest about his own struggles. More than that, he wants those who read his letter to be clear why he hasn't lost heart so they won't either.

In this section, Paul once again links his perseverance to his hope. Paul says there are three states someone who has put their faith in Jesus can be in. Each one gets progressively better.

The first state is living as a Christian in this fallen world. Paul describes this like living in a tent (v 1.). A tent isn't a permanent structure and neither are our bodies. The fabric of tents and of our bodies wastes away (4:16). We groan (vv. 2, 4), not only because of our struggles, but also because we long for the world beyond this one: a renewed creation in resurrection bodies (Rev. 21:1–4; 1 Cor. 15:42–44).

The second state is described in verses 6 to 8. If we die before the second coming of Jesus Christ, then we will not yet have our resurrection bodies, but we will be home with the Lord.

The third state is our permanent heavenly body. Paul describes this as being like a building rather than a tent (v. 1). No longer will those in the second state be disembodied, that is naked spirits (vv. 3–4). Instead, we will all be home with Jesus in bodies like his!

In the meantime, we have the Holy Spirit, as a deposit guaranteeing our future hope (v. 5). He also enables us to live lives that please Jesus (v. 9), ready for that day when we see him face to face and he gives his final verdict on how well we lived for him (v. 10).

REFLECTION

List as many things as you can that excite you about being home with Jesus in the new creation. Praise God for your hope!

DAY 12

READ 2 Corinthians 5:11–21

In these verses, we find the core convictions which underpinned Paul's entire ministry. Paul lived as an ambassador for Jesus, taking his gospel message into a hostile world (vv. 18–20).

Paul has been building up to these words since 2:14, when he broke off from explaining how he tried to meet up with Titus in Macedonia (a story he will pick up again in 7:5). Instead, he gave the Corinthians a fuller understanding of why he ministered in the way that he did. Paul's big point in defending his ministry is effectively: 'It's not about me; it's all about Jesus.' This is because:

1. Only Jesus will accurately judge our lives (vv. 11–13)

Being judged by Jesus (5:10) is at the forefront of Paul's thinking in these verses. There is a right fear of the Lord, even for Christians, when we understand Jesus sees, knows and accurately weighs every moment of our lives. But it is a liberating fear, because it frees us from the fear of man. What others think of us – whether they approve of us or think we are insane – doesn't change Jesus' verdict.

2. Only Jesus died and rose again that others might truly live (vv. 14–15)

It is only because Jesus died, while we were sinners and spiritually dead, that we can now live. Those who trust in him are raised to life with Christ.

3. Only Jesus can make people new creations (vv. 16–17)

Jesus was far more than just an ordinary man. In his resurrection body, he is the start of a new creation. In him, we are new creations – eternally bound to him. He is our true identity.

REFLECTION

Like Paul, we need to get people to take their eyes off us and focus on Jesus. Ask God for the grace to do that without fear.

DAY 13

READ 2 Corinthians 5:21

In the previous devotion, we didn't touch directly on this verse because it is worthy of a lifetime of meditation all on its own! There is so much of the content of the gospel, the message of reconciliation (v. 18), in this one verse that we will briefly consider each phrase.

'God made ...'

The initiative for our reconciliation didn't begin with us but with God. It is his plan of salvation. Ephesians 1:4 tells us God had it in his mind to rescue us even before he created the world.

'... him who had no sin ...'

Jesus was an utterly unique human being. Since the Fall (Gen. 3), every one of Adam's descendants has been born in sin. We sin because we are sinners. Our sinful behaviour reveals what is already in our hearts. But not Jesus! He was born of a virgin by the power of the Holy Spirit (Luke 1:26–38). He was the Son of God, whose consistently holy behaviour showed the perfect submission in his heart to the will of his Father.

'... to be sin for us ...'

This is the great exchange that took place on the cross. Jesus took all of our sin upon himself, as he bore the punishment we deserve and substituted his life for ours. He died in our place, paying the price in full for our sin (Rom. 5:6–8 and 6:23). Isaiah, writing 700 years before Jesus came, saw it clearly: 'he was pierced for our transgressions, he was crushed for our iniquities' (Is. 53:5).

'... so that in him we might become the righteousness of God'

The good news of the gospel isn't just that Jesus died on the cross to save us from hell, but that through his death and resurrection we can be reconciled to the God who made us. How? Because Jesus is able to include us in his perfect righteousness. So instead of seeing us as sinners in Adam, God now looks on us as righteous in his Son. He sees us as if we have never sinned and will never sin ever again. Hallelujah!

REFLECTION

Commit this verse to memory and give thanks for the reconciling power of the gospel.

DAY 14

READ 2 Corinthians 6:1–13

2 Corinthians is Paul's most personal letter. As we've seen repeatedly, and as Paul spells out in verses 11 to 13, he opens up his heart to the believers in Corinth again and again. He does that because the church has often rejected his Apostleship and is chasing after more impressive leaders.

Therefore Paul wants them to understand his motivation as a minister of the new covenant and to recognise the outworking of that in the way he lives. Paul knows that if the gospel doesn't change the way the Corinthians live, then they haven't received Jesus at all. To hear the gospel and not respond to it daily is to receive God's grace in vain (v. 1).

Today, the gospel isn't just good news for those who first turn to Christ, but for us all as we continually do battle with sin. We seek to live out our new righteousness in Jesus through his life-transforming grace (v. 2).

So what marks out Paul as a man who has genuinely received the Word of God and therefore as a leader worth following?

1. He is prepared to suffer for the sake of the gospel (vv. 4–5)

Jesus told his disciples to take up their cross daily and follow him (Mt. 16:24). Paul takes these words seriously and follows the way of his master. Jesus suffered in the ways Paul describes here.

2. He is walking in holiness for the sake of the gospel (vv. 6–7)

So often the gospel is discredited by ministers who don't practise what they preach. Paul is determined, by the power of the Holy Spirit, to live a life and conduct his ministry in ways consistent with the gospel message.

3. He is sacrificing personal comfort for the sake of the gospel (vv. 8–10)

Paul sacrifices his reputation, his popularity, his health, his rights, his happiness and his financial security to make Jesus known.

REFLECTION

What is it costing you to follow Jesus? Ask the Holy Spirit to convict you of ways you can more consistently live out the gospel in your life.

DAY 15

READ 2 Corinthians 6:14 – 7:1

Paul desperately wants to restore the relationship between himself and the believers in Corinth. This isn't because he is needy and can't handle their rejection emotionally, but because he is convinced his way of life and pattern of ministry are what Christ demands of all who truly belong to him. If the Corinthians pursue more impressive leaders, who don't live humble, gospel-centred lives as Jesus did, then Paul thinks they will have received the gospel in vain (6:1). So having summed up his life as a servant of God (6:3–10), Paul concludes this whole section on living under the new covenant with an appeal to the Corinthians to live wholeheartedly for the Lord (7:1).

If they are going to live for Jesus, it is imperative that they don't partner with those who don't know him. 6:14–16 can be applied to marriage and to some business arrangements, but primarily these verses are a warning to believers not to bind themselves to leaders who don't live as Jesus did. The yoke bound oxen together so they walked in step. But, Paul asks in these verses, how can someone who knows Jesus walk in step with someone who doesn't – whose heart is still wicked, who is still living in darkness, who is working for Satan (Belial is a Jewish name for Satan) and who still serves idols?

Instead, Paul calls the believers in Corinth to separate themselves from those people that they might be distinctive, living holy lives in the power of the Spirit and trusting in God's Word (6:16-18). Paul reminds the believers that they are the temple of the living God, the place where God dwells on earth by his Spirit. He then quotes promises from the Old Testament (Lev. 26:12; Jer. 32:38; Ezek. 37:27), where God promises to be with his people and father them. All these promises are ours in Jesus!

REFLECTION

Holy living requires that we say 'no' to everything that would contaminate our body and spirit, and 'yes' to everything that will make us more like Jesus. Ask the Spirit to help you to do this today.

DAY 16

READ 2 Corinthians 7:2–16

These verses are the emotional peak of 2 Corinthians. Paul has been brought as low as he thinks he could go through the troubles he faces in his current ministry and his ongoing conflict with the believers in Corinth (1:8–9). Following a further bad report from Corinth of renewed hostility towards him, Paul will be filled with righteous anger in chapters 10 to 13. But in these verses in chapter 7 Paul is full of joy! What has made the difference?

Verses 5 to 7 tell us that Paul has finally met up with Titus (see 2:12–13). Titus has returned from Corinth with positive news. As Paul has prayed repeatedly, the believers have made room for him in their hearts (v. 2) and have repented over their rejection of his ministry and the gospel he preached. What evidence does Paul see of their repentance?

1. They made Titus welcome (vv. 7, 13–15)
The comfort and refreshment they brought to Titus were fruit not only of their love for him, but of their relationship with Jesus Christ. True repentance increases our love for others.

2. They took Paul's words seriously (vv. 8–9)
The Corinthians were affected by Paul's third letter (lost to us, but sent between 1 and 2 Corinthians). They were cut to the heart. Because Paul was an Apostle, he wrote with God's authority. True repentance is always a heartfelt response to God's Word.

3. Their behaviour changed (vv. 10–11)
Instead of attacking Paul, the Corinthian believers wanted to prove their own obedience to God's ways. True repentance leads to renewed obedience.

All of this fills Paul with a deep joy (vv. 4, 7). He has always loved the Corinthians. The whole of this letter (for example, v. 3) shows that love. Wonderfully for Paul that love is now mutual (v. 7). His confidence in the Corinthian believers has not been misplaced (vv. 4, 14, 16). They are partners once again in the great work of the gospel.

REFLECTION

Give thanks to God for those who inspire you in your own walk with Jesus.

DAY 17

READ 2 Corinthians 8:1–9

Paul, having heard from Titus that the relationship between himself and the Corinthians was restored, begins a new section in this letter. In chapters 8 and 9 he wants the Corinthians to express their faith in Jesus and their partnership in the gospel with him by generously giving to a collection for the poor Christians living in Judea. In the months the church had been at odds with Paul, they had failed to make good on previous promises (8:10-11). Paul now gives them the opportunity to put this matter right.

Paul begins by focusing on giving as an act of grace (vv. 1, 6–7). By nature, we are selfish, especially with our money. In Christ, we can grow in rich generosity.

Paul presents the Corinthians with an outstanding example of this grace: the Macedonian churches (v. 1). We know Paul experienced some of the greatest trials he had ever faced as he suffered alongside the believers in Macedonia (1:8–9; 7:5), but he also experienced boundless joy (7:4). Part of that joy was undoubtedly the insistence of the Macedonian believers that, despite their extreme poverty, they gave generously to the collection for the believers in Judea (vv. 3-4). Paul saw that as evidence of their good-heartedness before the Lord and their love for him (v. 5).

Paul therefore sent Titus to Corinth to urge those believers to do the same (v. 6) and to grow in this grace of giving as they had in so many other areas (v. 7).

His ultimate example to the church is not the Macedonian Christians but our Lord Jesus Christ (vv. 8–9). Paul reminds the believers in Corinth of the gospel. Christ exchanged the glory of heaven for the anguish of the cross. This was so that through his death we might exchange our shame and condemnation for his righteous life. When it comes to the grace of giving, we cannot outgive our God. He gave everything for us.

REFLECTION

Look over your spending for the past month. Does that show a generous attitude towards God? Ask Jesus for more of the grace of giving.

DAY 18

READ 2 Corinthians 8:10–15

In the first nine verses of this chapter, Paul considered how a rich generosity is a gracious outworking of the gospel in believers' lives. As we sacrificially give to those in desperate material need, it is a picture of the self-giving love that took Jesus to the cross to rescue us in our desperate spiritual need. Giving provides an opportunity to grow more like our Saviour. That's why Paul calls it grace! Only the Spirit of God can make us more like Jesus.

In these verses, Paul looks at three other dimensions of godly giving: desire, devotion and dependence.

Verses 10 to 12 focus on the desire to give. When the believers in Corinth rejected Paul and the gospel he preached, they lost their desire to make good on their promises of the previous year to help the poor in Judea. Now they are back in fellowship, Paul expects them to have an 'eager willingness' (v. 11) to contribute to the collection. The acceptability of the gift would not depend on the amount given, which would inevitably vary according to their means, but the willingness of the heart behind it.

Verses 13 and 14 both underline that Paul's goal in collecting this gift is equality between the Christians inside and outside of Judea. The predominantly Jewish believers in Judea would benefit materially from the predominantly Gentile believers in Asia. This type of devotion between Jews and Gentiles was unthinkable before Christ's death brought believers from all nations together as one family.

Verse 15 applies an Old Testament principle from Exodus 16:18 that in times of both plenty and need, there are opportunities for believers to learn greater dependence upon Jesus. If we have more than we need, we should be actively looking for opportunities to give. If we have less than we need, we should be actively praying for Jesus to supply our needs. In both situations, we are showing we love, trust and find comfort in Christ more than we love, trust and find comfort in money.

REFLECTION

How does your life show the desire for, the devotion to and the dependence upon Jesus that Paul writes about here?

DAY 19

READ 2 Corinthians 8:16 – 9:5

Paul faced many false allegations from his critics in Corinth. Some of these were about the way he funded his ministry. Aware of his critics (8:20), Paul is at pains to underline his integrity and that of his ministry team in their plan to administer the gift for the poor believers in Judea (8:16–23). Once Paul has done that, he then challenges the Corinthians about their own integrity (8:24 – 9:5).

Paul defines integrity in 8:21. It involves doing the right thing before God (who sees the motives of our hearts) and doing the right thing before other people (who see how we act).

Paul highlights three men who will take the lead on collecting the gifts from the churches in Asia and ensuring they are given to the believers in Judea. The first is Titus (8:16–17, 23), who has recently returned from Corinth, refreshed and full of love for them. He is keen to return to complete the collection of their gift. With him will come two unnamed brothers (8:18–19, 22), the first of whom Paul underlines has also been chosen by the churches. These men have proven their integrity before God and before his people (8:23).

What about the Corinthians? Paul wants them to demonstrate their love (8:24) by stepping up and giving the financial help they had enthusiastically promised the previous year (9:1–2). If they do that, it will be a sign their hearts are right with God. Paul wants to avoid the embarrassment of arriving in Corinth and finding them unprepared, so he has sent his advanced party to ensure this doesn't happen (9:3–5). His integrity, as well as that of the Corinthian believers, is at stake.

REFLECTION

Ask the Holy Spirit to search your heart, as David does in Psalm 139:23–24, and to bring to mind any areas in your own finances where you are not acting with integrity.

DAY 20

READ 2 Corinthians 9:6–15

Paul concludes this section on giving with an appeal to the Corinthians to be joyfully generous (vv. 6–7). Don Carson's sermon on The Gospel Coalition website is quite brilliantly titled, 'Laughing all the way from the bank'. That sums up the spirit of these final verses. As we give generously with joy in our hearts, God blesses us and others through us. Here Paul gives us three compelling reasons to be joyfully generous.

1. We can depend upon God as we give (vv. 8–11)

Verse 8 reminds us of an essential truth: 'God is able'. He has *all* the grace we need. He has control over *all* things at *all* times. So he is able to supply *all* that we need to complete *all* the good works he has prepared in advance for us to do (Eph. 2:10). Verse 9, quoting Psalm 122:9, reminds us that whatever we give is from God and his ultimate purpose is to display his righteousness in our lives. Verses 10 and 11 underline these same truths. As we depend upon our heavenly Father, our lives more fully reflect the righteous life of his perfect Son.

2. Others can give thanks to God for our gifts (vv. 12–14)

Verse 11 ended by saying the gifts given would 'result in thanksgiving to God'. The idea behind the collection for the churches in Judea was to alleviate their sufferings, but it would achieve far more than that. It would thrill the hearts of the believers who received the gift because it would be a sign of God's work in the lives of the Corinthians.

3. All of us can give thanks to God for his gift (v. 15)

Whatever we give, God has given more. Whatever our faith costs us, God has paid a higher price. His gift to us, the gift of his one and only Son, is beyond description. His self-giving, joyful, generous love to us in Jesus should cause us to praise our God and put our money where our mouth is.

REFLECTION

Give thanks to God for his gift of Jesus Christ. List as many blessings as you can that you have generously been given in him.

DAY 21

READ 2 Corinthians 10:1–6

Chapter 10 marks the start of a new section which runs all the way to the end of the letter. Once again Paul is forced to defend his ministry.

There is a lot of debate about why, having seemingly been joyfully reconciled with the Corinthians in chapter 7, so soon afterwards there has been a further breakdown in the relationship. Perhaps the most likely explanation is that having written chapters 1 to 9, Paul received new information about a group of so-called 'super-apostles' (11:5) who were seeking to undermine not only Paul's ministry but the outworking of the gospel among the Corinthians. This was so serious that as Paul concludes his letter, he challenges those in Corinth to examine themselves 'to see whether you are in the faith' (13:5). No wonder he is at his most passionate in these four chapters! The eternal destiny of these people whom he cares so much about is at stake.

Right at the start of chapter 10 we can see the outline of the accusations against Paul. The style and substance of his apostolic ministry are attacked. He is accused of being bold in his writing but timid in person (v. 1; also 10:10–11). His critics say he claims to be living for Christ but actually is living 'by the standards of this world' (v. 2). Verse 7a highlights that the critics are judging Paul on the wrong criteria.

In these verses, we can also begin to see how Paul will deal with these criticisms. He will continue to display the character of Christ, in all his seeming weakness (v. 1). He will continue to use the power of the gospel (1 Cor. 1:21-24), not any worldly power, to break down every evil stronghold and every false idea, until 'every thought' is aligned with the gospel of Christ (vv. 3–5). For those who reject this correction, they can expect to be disciplined when the Apostle Paul comes in person (v. 6; also 13:2–4). This is a battle for the soul of this church that Paul is simply not prepared to lose.

REFLECTION

Are you unfairly judgemental of your church leaders or do you judge them on the wrong criteria? Repent if needs be. Give thanks for Christ's work in and through them.

DAY 22

READ 2 Corinthians 10:7–18

As we have already seen, critics in Corinth are challenging both the style and the substance of Paul's ministry. Paul had thought these issues had been laid to rest (7:6–7), but a new group of so-called 'super-apostles' have arrived in Corinth and are rubbing salt into re-opened wounds. In these verses, Paul explains five foundational principles that underpin all of his work for Jesus.

1. Confident in Christ (vv. 7–8)
Paul wants to remind the Corinthians that he belongs to Christ in the special apostolic way his critics are so quick to claim for themselves. Paul's authority to deal with these persistent difficulties in Corinth comes from his confidence that he is doing the work that the Lord gave him to build up the church.

2. Consistent in ministry (vv. 9–11)
Paul's detractors are attacking his style. They say there is a gulf between the force of his letters and the weakness of his rhetoric. Paul replies that those in Corinth could expect another painful visit if they would not repent in response to his writing. He would be consistent in his approach to their sin.

3. (No!) Comparison with others (vv. 12–15)
Paul declares that comparing our lives with others is foolish and claiming their work as our own is wrong. His critics do both these things. Instead, Paul says we should delight in the work God has entrusted to us. We can then boast in the work we see Jesus doing in others' lives, as Paul does (7:14).

4. Continuation in mission (vv. 15–16)
Paul's motivation in reconciling with the Corinthians is not just a matter of harmony among the Christian family, but to open the possibility of further mission beyond Corinth. He wants to use the church as a launch pad for the gospel, as he boldly goes where no man has gone before with the good news about Jesus.

5. Commended by Christ (vv. 17–18)
Paul will only boast in Christ. He is living for the Lord's final commendation of his life and to hear him say, 'Well done!' (Mt. 25:21).

REFLECTION

Think about the work Jesus wants you to do for him. Are your foundations the same as Paul's?

DAY 23

READ 2 Corinthians 11:1–15

In the face of renewed criticism, Paul defends his ministry saying he will fight back with the power of the gospel (10:1–6) and with unwavering loyalty to the cause of Christ his Lord (10:7–18).

In chapter 11, Paul moves from defence to offence! He says that he wants to 'cut the ground from under those' who claim for themselves the same apostolic authority Christ has given to him (v. 12). To do so, he levels three serious charges against them.

1. His critics work for Satan not Christ (vv. 2–3, 13–15)

Paul works for Christ. Throughout the letters to the Corinthians it is clear Paul loves this church like a father loves his child. In verse 2 he says he acts like a father trying to stop his teenage daughter breaking off her engagement and running off with an unworthy man. He is jealous for the honour of this church. He wants them to be totally devoted to Jesus, wholly his.

But just as Satan deceived Eve (v. 3; Gen. 3:1–6), so Paul says these so-called 'super-apostles' are deceiving the Corinthians. Just as Satan seemed to be offering something better than the life God promised, so Paul says these men are servants of the Evil One, drawing the Corinthians away from the true life God promised through Christ.

2. His critics want adulation not Christ (vv. 4–6)

Paul's critics pride themselves on the power of their public speaking. They gain adulation from the quality of their performance. As an untrained speaker, Paul's speeches may be less impressive, but at the heart of what he proclaims is the gospel and the glory of Jesus. These other men are distorting the gospel message by glorifying themselves.

3. His critics love money not Christ (vv. 7–11)

Paul's critics usually measure success by how much someone is paid. They love money. Paul, out of love for Christ and the Corinthians, does not ask for money when he preaches the gospel, but lives from the gifts he collected from the Macedonian churches.

REFLECTION

God wants all of us to have a pure devotion to Christ. Confess any areas of your life where you have been straying from him.

DAY 24

READ 2 Corinthians 11:16–33

Having underlined his allegiance to Christ in chapter 10, and having exposed his critics in the first half of chapter 11 as masqueraders working for the cause of Satan, Paul now fights them on their own turf: the field of boasting.

Paul's enemies love to boast of their accomplishments. They focus on triumphant moments in their ministries. Paul, reaching out in love to the Corinthian church, decides to play them at their own game. However, as we shall see, none of the pieces he puts on the board are anything like those used by his opponents.

Verses 16 to 21, and Paul's comment in parentheses in verse 23, show how toe-curling Paul finds engaging in this way. He considers it utterly foolish. But because the Corinthians are surrendering to such dangerous men, who are exploitative and spiritually abusive, Paul goes into battle for their souls.

His opening lines in verses 21 to 23 look as if he is teeing off to out-boast his enemies in terms of his own accomplishments. Paul underscores his Jewish credentials and his devotion to Christ. Following his phrase 'I have worked much harder', maybe we would expect him to recount stories of souls won, churches planted and money raised. But no! Paul goes where his opponents would never go and lists all his weakest moments. In verses 23 to 25, he details all the times he was punished for his faith. Verses 25 to 26 record the dangers he has been in as he travelled sharing the gospel. Verse 27 shows how living for Christ has almost broken him physically. Verses 28 and 29 highlight the daily emotional cost Paul has borne of interceding for those afflicted by suffering and sin. Finally, in verses 30 to 33, he draws his boasting to an end by telling another story which shamed him. In Damascus, a city where once he was held in high esteem, he was forced to flee (Acts 9:23–25).

All this makes it clear that suffering, not accomplishments, adorns the lives of those who are truly serving Christ.

REFLECTION

Reflect on how much Jesus suffered for you. Ask his Spirit to make you willing to suffer for the cause of the gospel.

DAY 25

READ 2 Corinthians 12:1–10

Many people love to boast about their spiritual experiences. We can be sure Paul's critics in Corinth did. From 1 Corinthians 11–14 we know that the Corinthian church was obsessed with dramatic signs of the Holy Spirit's power and therefore likely to be impressed by these 'super-apostles'. Out of love for the Lord and his people, Paul humbly shares something of his own experience of God, putting the focus on not the extraordinary visions he has received, but the ongoing sufficiency of God's daily grace.

Paul is a wonderful example of meekness. Where his enemies boast to impress others, Paul's great concern is that others will think too highly of him (v. 6). Even though he has experienced the 'third heaven' (vv. 2–4) – another way of saying the highest heaven, where Jesus dwells with his people (Luke 23:43) – Paul will not boast of such experiences. He even puts them into the third person to distance himself from them, saying, 'I know a man in Christ' rather than directly talking about himself. How humble!

Instead, in verses 7 to 10, Paul owns the experience of prolonged suffering yet knowing God's sufficient grace. Having seen heaven fourteen years previously, Paul was afflicted from then on with 'a thorn in my flesh' (v. 7). Nobody knows exactly what this thorn was, but it must have been unbearable to have troubled the man who went through all the sufferings of 11:23–33. Three prolonged times Paul prayed for God to take away this affliction and three times he received the same answer: 'My grace is sufficient for you, for my power is made perfect in weakness' (v. 9). Paul therefore says he will boast about his weaknesses because through them the power of Jesus can be seen more clearly in his life.

When my first wife, Elaine, was dying of cancer, we saw this same grace at work in her life. We prayed daily for her healing, but instead God gave her the grace to testify to his goodness throughout her terminal illness. Hallelujah! What a Saviour!

REFLECTION

Think about your weaknesses. Thank God that every one of them gives you the opportunity to rely on Jesus' strength.

DAY 26

READ 2 Corinthians 12:11–21

In these verses, Paul's reluctant boasting has come to an end. He feels foolish boasting (v. 11), but has been driven to it by the danger the church in Corinth faces from the so-called 'super-apostles'. Now, as he nears the end of this letter, he prepares the Corinthians for a third personal visit (v. 14). The question that hangs in the air is how will he be received? Will this be another painful visit (2:1)? Or would the Corinthian church repent, as they had following Paul's previous letter (2:3–4) and the visit of Titus (7:5–13), so Paul could anticipate a joyful reunion with them?

For that to happen, there are three negative truths that the Corinthian believers must grasp.

1. Paul is not inferior to the so-called 'super-apostles' (vv. 11–12)

The church in Corinth is obsessed with outward signs of spiritual authority and power (1 Cor. 11–14). The 'super-apostles' show off their own power, but Paul demonstrates God's power. This includes signs, which point to Christ; wonders, which provoke awe towards God; and mighty, miraculous works, which reveal the Spirit's power.

2. Paul is not exploitative towards the Corinthian church (vv. 13–18)

The church in Corinth is foolishly impressed by how much the 'super-apostles' demand from them in exchange for their services. Paul has his head in his hands at their stupidity! He loves this church as if they were his own children, so he refuses payment from them. Instead, Paul, and all those he has sent to Corinth, give everything out of love to the church without charge. They are not exploitative; they are generous.

3. Paul is not satisfied with the Corinthians' shallow repentance (vv. 19–21)

In everything Paul has done, he has sought to strengthen this wayward church. However, their repentance has been shallow. Verse 20 returns to issues raised in 1 Corinthians 1–4; verse 21 to issues raised in 1 Corinthians 5–7. For all Paul's efforts, has anything really changed?

REFLECTION

Think about those sins that regularly trip you up. Confess them. Thank God for his forgiveness. Ask him for renewed grace to follow Jesus.

DAY 27

READ 2 Corinthians 13:1–14

As Paul signs off his letter, he prepares the church for another personal visit (v. 1). But will he find the church full of repentance and faith, or rebellion and falsehood?

If the latter is true, then Paul says he will deal with those who are proven to have sinned (vv. 1–2). His critics accuse him of being imposing in his writing yet unimpressive in person (10:10–11), but here Paul further substantiates his claim that he will be in person exactly as he is in his writing. When he visits, Paul is confident Christ will speak powerfully through him to deal with any sin in the Corinthian church (vv. 3–4). He is willing to serve the church by disciplining those who live in rebellion to the gospel of Christ.

But his hope for his third visit is quite different (v. 10). Paul desires that the believers will examine themselves for evidence that they belong to Christ (vv. 5–6), then repent of any wrongdoing and instead strive for perfection in Christ (vv. 7–9). Paul longs that maturity, which has been lacking in this church ever since he planted it about six years previously, would finally be their experience. Every good parent wants their child to grow up to be a responsible adult. Paul wants his spiritual children in Corinth to grow up to be like Christ.

So, as he briefly says 'cheerio', verses 11 to 13 make a final appeal to their hearts. Paul urges them to aim for Christlikeness in all things. Be joyful. Be encouraging. Be unified in mind and daily living. Experience, then share, the love and peace of God, which must characterise relationships within the local church and between true believers everywhere.

How could a church as flawed as the one in Corinth do these things? How can we? Not in our own strength, but by drawing from the inexhaustible well of grace, love and power lavished on us by our triune God (v. 14).

REFLECTION

Pray verse 14 would be your own daily experience, as the life-transforming grace of Jesus Christ continues its powerful, loving work in you and in your church family.

Neil Todman
2 CORINTHIANS
LIFE-TRANSFORMING GRACE
27 UNDATED DEVOTIONS THROUGH THE BOOK OF 2 CORINTHIANS